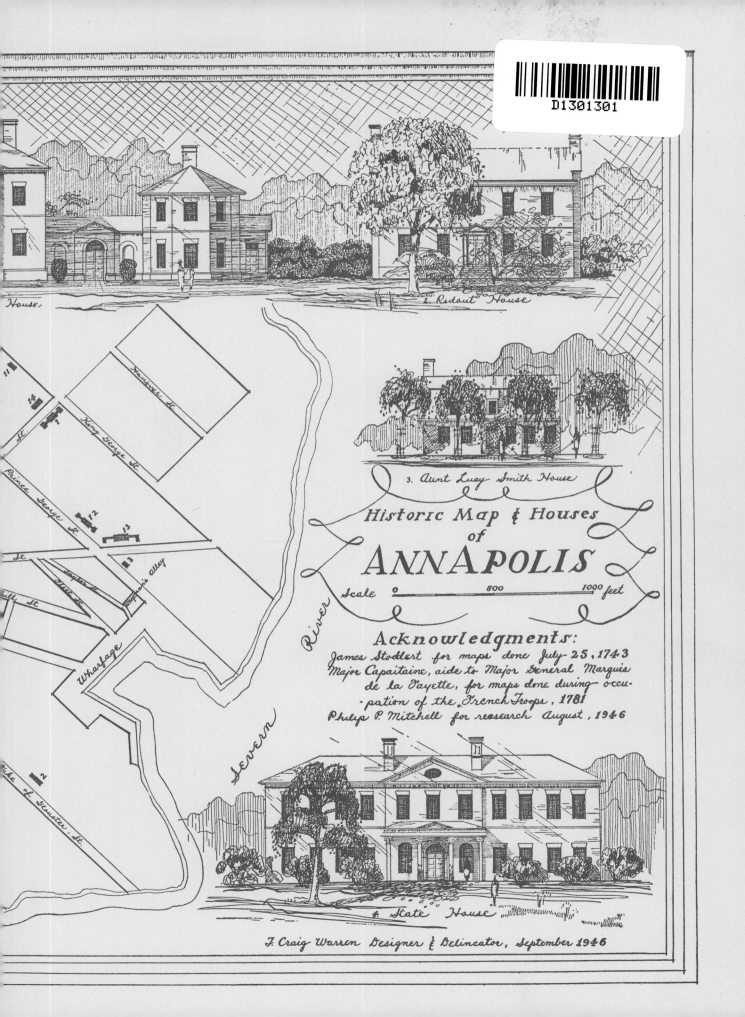

2. Redout House

3. Aunt Lucy Smith House

Historic Map & Houses
of
ANNAPOLIS

Scale 0 ——— 500 ——— 1000 feet

Acknowledgments:
James Stoddert for maps done July 25, 1743
Major Capaitaine, aide to Major General Marquis
de la Fayette, for maps done during occu-
pation of the French Troops, 1781
Philip P. Mitchell for research August, 1946

4. State House

F. Craig Warren Designer & Delineator, September 1946

The Entrance of the Hammond-Harwood House

ANNAPOLIS HOUSES

1700=1775

By · DEERING · DAVIS · A · I · D ·

Foreword by
JOSEPH · MULLEN · A · I · D ·

BONANZA BOOKS · NEW YORK

AUTHOR'S NOTE

THERE HAS BEEN MUCH recent discussion between the authorities at the United States Naval Academy and those of St. John's College concerning the enlargement of the Academy at the expense of destroying the present College buildings. As of the moment, St. John's has won its point but now there are disturbing rumors that the Naval Academy is planning to expand into the town itself. That would result in the destruction of buildings, even more important architecturally and historically, than those on the College Green. With what may lie ahead in mind, no true American would wish the Academy to be deprived of anything really necessary to its work, but thinking backward to the heritage of American tradition, which its graduates will be defending (if war should come again) it does seem that these surviving tangible links with our country's past should be preserved, if possible. On the other side of a narrow river there is an abundance of vacant land. To the United States Navy, of all organizations, some sort of over water transportation should be a small problem.

The Cadets of the Academy gain much, at least subconsciously, by their four years of association with the homes of our Colonial progenitors. To this end, instead of further destruction—too many fine buildings which formerly stood on the present Academy grounds have already been sacrificed—every effort should be made to preserve and restore all that remains. So many of the early structures have been carelessly and thoughtlessly defaced by alterations. This is especially true of many buildings now used as shops. As a final word of encouragement in urging a restoration movement: real estate values in Annapolis are comparatively reasonable.

The author has attempted to show in this volume no dwellings that have had their original character changed, though of course some minor alterations are sometimes unavoidably apparent.

In closing—a few words of appreciation. My thanks are due, above all, to the owners of the houses shown—to the librarians who aided so greatly in collecting the material, whether historical or pictorial—notably to Miss Virginia Daiker, Mrs. C. Denman, Mrs. Clara E. LeGear, Mr. William Davis, and to Mr. Hugh Clark, all of the Library of Congress; to Miss Mercedes Jordan of the K Street Library—to Mrs. Margaret Kemp, Miss Patricia Randles, and my wife, Evelyn Davis, whose unfailing patience, humor and good judgment transformed my rough notes into printable form, and to Jack Bird for his wonderful retouching of some of the illustrations, and to Mr. Harry C. Ellsworth.

DEERING DAVIS

TABLE OF CONTENTS

LIST OF ILLUSTRATIONS

EARLY HISTORY OF ANNAPOLIS

ANYONE FAMILIAR with Maryland and Virginia is conscious of the usually good-natured but intense rivalry between the two states. This spirit of competition has endured from Colonial Times when it reached its zenith. A history of Maryland's capital would not be complete without constant references to Williamsburg, for so long Virginia's seat of government. A treatise on the early architecture of Annapolis has even more need for constant reference to its neighboring rival executive city. Mr. Rockefeller's wonderful generosity in so superbly restoring Colonial Williamsburg has made its beauties familiar to all. To take advantage of this great educational work, a frank comparison between Annapolis and Williamsburg seems the intelligent method of presenting at least a part of the subject matter of this volume. It is to be hoped that this comparison does not bring the ancient rivalry to open warfare but that the competitive spirit among the antiquarians of the two states is aroused and through their efforts new and fascinating facts unearthed.

The first settlers near the mouth of the Severn were a group of militant Puritans who migrated to Maryland in the 1640's at the suggestion of the Virginia authorities. They called this area Providence. Within a few years a tiny settlement sprang up on the peninsula and was known as Anne Arundel Town, both the town and county deriving the name from the second Lord Baltimore's wife.

Soon after his arrival in 1693, the second Royal Governor, Sir Francis Nicholson, decided that St. Mary's, the capital at that time, was too inaccessible for the fast growing province. Despite vigorous objection on the part of landholders in and near St. Mary's he declared, through the Assembly, that Anne Arundel Town, a village of forty tiny houses, only three of which were brick, should henceforth be the seat of government and be re-named Annapolis, in honor of Princess Anne, later Queen of England. The first meeting of the Assembly took place on February 28, 1695, in one of the three brick houses, the home of Major Edward Dorsey, which still stands, though greatly enlarged and sadly altered.

Williamsburg, at first a settlement in the area known as the "Pallisades," in 1633 was called Middle Plantation. In 1699 by Act of Assembly, it was decided to move the seat of authority from Jamestown to this village which was re-named Williamsburg, in deference to William III.

Annapolis, then, is a few years senior to its rival as a capital. Both cities were formally planned as seats of government. The Virginia town was laid out on the familiar grid pattern with the Governor's Palace as the focal point. Governor Nicholson chose the much more unusual plan of streets radiating from two circles, one to contain the capital and the other, the Anglican church. This was the first instance in America of this type of Plat, later made so famous by Major L'Enfant in his scheme for the Nation's capital.

In 1708, Queen Anne granted a city charter to Annapolis. Williamsburg was not formally incorporated until 1722.

Sir Francis Nicholson, before coming to Maryland, had been Lieutenant Governor of Virginia, and in 1693 had helped found the famous and lovely William and Mary College, second only to Harvard as America's oldest higher seat of learning.*

Still existing is the Forensic Club, one of several Annapolis men's clubs in Colonial days.

* Once more, his interest in education led to prompt results. In 1696, King William's School in Annapolis was established, continuing under that name until it became a part of St. John's College in 1784, a date which clearly establishes that latter institution as third in order of seniority amongst American seats of higher education.

Both capitals were laid out with approximately the same area, and from 1700 to 1776 kept an even pace in growth of population. Annapolis had 60 houses and 150 population in 1694; 374 inhabitants in 1696; 1217 in 1747; and about 3,000 with 450 houses in 1776. Both cities lay claim to having built the first theater. In fact, Annapolis records clearly indicate that three were erected before the Revolution, in: 1752, 1760, and 1771. However, the research done by the restoration group for Colonial Williamsburg shows that a playhouse there was completed as early as 1716. With all these similarities and rivalries, one fundamentally important *difference* was the decisive factor in their respective architectural achievements.

PLAN OF THE HARBOUR AND CITY OF ANNAPOLIS

The map on the facing page, though dealing more accurately with the surrounding country than the town itself, is included for its charm as a drawing and for the picture it gives of the town's setting during the approximate time covered in this volume.

The author believes that the map's designer was also the author of the "Frenchmen's Map" of Williamsburg which proved so great an aid in restoring that city. What a pity that this Annapolis Map was not also concentrated on the town itself!

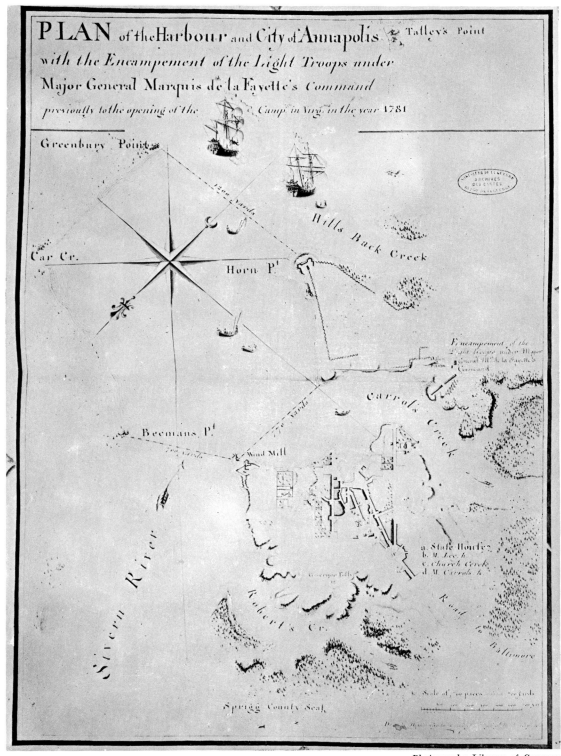

Map of Annapolis and its environs

ARCHITECTURE OF ANNAPOLIS

THE IMPORTANT basic difference between Colonial Annapolis and Colonial Williamsburg was that while both were state capitals the Maryland city was, prior to the Revolution, an extremely prosperous and important seaport. The Virginia town existed solely as the seat of government and the location of William and Mary College. Hence, its most important architecture consisted of the magnificent Governor's Palace, the State House, the University Buildings, Bruton Parish Church, plus a handful of "town houses" of simple unpretentious charm, the Raleigh, and other taverns. In 1742 Annapolis, prodded by Royal Governor Bladen, made an abortive attempt to produce a Governor's Palace of its own, but probably realizing the stupendous and costly effort of competing with the magnificent edifice at Williamsburg, soon lost interest so that it only succeeded in being known as Bladen's Folly, and after standing uncompleted for forty years, finally became McDowell Hall, the main building of St. John's College. A comparison of the other public buildings is difficult. St. Anne's, Annapolis' early church, no longer exists in Colonial form. However, there is every indication to show that it was a more ambitious structure than Bruton Parish Church at Williamsburg. The Maryland State House, much altered, still stands. Though no larger or finer, it is in the more sophisticated later architectural style than that of the Virginia city's capital. Williamsburg's significant architecture is the earlier by fifty years and belongs to the Wren, Queen Anne, Early Georgian style. The Governor's Palace completely dominates the scene both actually and in its influence on American architectural development, especially the Virginian plantation houses of the first half of the 18th Century. Annapolis has a few simple remaining examples of this earlier style. Some of these have the gambrel roof so prevalent in early Maryland building. Unfortunately lack of care and unsightly additions have spoiled too many. Much careful restoration should be done, especially in the case of the old shops now spoiled by modern windows and false fronts.

By 1765 the Maryland town's importance as a thriving seaport, as well as the seat of government, gave the aristocratic and wealthy plantation owners an excuse to have built "town houses" of considerable magnificence which they occupied from November to April or May, and from which they conducted their business affairs in connection with shipping, etc. No doubt their wives and daughters had considerable influence in starting this movement to the city, and just as surely in engendering the spirit of rivalry among the "Great Names" of Maryland to outdo one another in the opulence of these town residences. Thus, the most important architecture belongs to late Georgian style.

During the decade, 1765-1775, six private dwellings were constructed in Annapolis which, for sophistication of architectural design and superb detail both exterior and interior, reached a point of perfection scarcely equalled elsewhere on this continent before or since. A most fortunate chain of circumstances and events has preserved all six of these to the present time, although four of them should most certainly be restored to their original beauty, having been marred by thoughtless "improvements" during the last two hundred years.

It is an extraordinary fact that of these six houses, three were of the five-part type, the acknowledged zenith of the formal plan while elsewhere in all the Colonies there were not more than a dozen other examples of this design. After the Revolution a comparatively large number were built and many of the earlier houses were converted to the five-part type by the addition of wings and passages, or in many cases simply connecting already symmetrically placed dependencies by means of hyphens. This is the case at beautiful Virginia "Westover" whose connecting links are only about fifty years old.

Another striking difference between the two capitals, architecturally, is the universal use in Annapolis of extremely handsome wooden entrance doors while there were none at Williamsburg or, indeed, in all Virginia other than the portals at Wilton on the James, and Gadsby's Tavern in Alexandria.

Several of the great mansions of Annapolis had their own water frontage and, others though located in town were of country architectural style, each set in a miniature park of four or five acres. The structures themselves were erected so that one entered directly from the street, leaving the entire property at the garden side of the house. Here were superb formally planted terraces falling gradually to the water, but also vegetable gardens, stables and slave quarters, in fact the complete equipment of a self-sustaining manorial estate in miniature. Unfortunately no such complete entourage remains and at least one should be restored to serve as an example. In Williamsburg, the Wythe House with its dependencies offers a perfect illustration.

Famous 18th Century prototypes of this garden-dwelling plan existed at Versailles. There one still finds exquisite diminutive chateaux, each with its lovely walled courtyard and garden. Another, almost unique French rather than English design characteristic, was the custom of having a living room of the house on the second floor overlooking the garden. The maisons de ville at Versailles universally follow this scheme.

The simple and factual way to correctly visualize this resplendent Colonial city and to understand its great cultural prestige, in spite of its small size, is to realize that it held the same position in 1775 as today is occupied by extremely fashionable suburban towns near our great metropolitan areas where a few semi-country show places owned by the very rich, completely dominate the local scene.

FOREWORD

ANNAPOLIS—Annapolis—Annapolis—a name thrice blessed and thrice proven. A name which awakens memories and meanings of varied import to many and various people in our country. A city which means a number of things to numbers of people. So rich is the connotation of the character of the gracious little city of Annapolis that it is a fascinating and confusing task to know where to begin to think of it.

It is like a brilliant top—spinning in its own integrity of historical significance. And it has been spinning so since its first founding.

This many faceted little city is known and honoured for many reasons, to name a few at random first as the capital of Maryland and the attendant gracious pattern of living which has prevailed since it was first presided over by the Royal Governor; for its outstanding place in the history of American shipping; for the cultural background of the founding in *1696* of St. John's College which has endured and maintained its high standards of education through the years; for the Academy which is the Alma Mater of all officers of the U. S. Navy and is just now celebrating its centennial; and for its present-day aspect of a thriving American community. Behind all these many facets has been a steadfast pattern—and it is with this that we are most concerned in this volume—a steadfast pattern of gracious living which most properly exemplifies an expression of dignified American life.

Most specifically are we interested with a sure and fine vein of architecture which has found expression in the homes in and near Annapolis. For it is the homes—their design and proportion and detail which set the tenor of the manner of living in any community.

As we stand, as we do now, at the end of a period of war, and at the end of a period where there has been very little building, either industrial or domestic, for the better part of two decades, we are in a position to look around us in the field of architecture. We *must* look around us, we must look into the future to see what we want, we must look into the immediate past and into the distant past.

We must consider thoughtfully to know if it is something new which we will be wanting or if perhaps we already have the pattern best suited to a permanent way of life in our country. It may be that there is in a pattern—ready made, ready proven in various scales for our future living—domestically—at least.

The ancient belief that where there is a demand there is a supply is again evinced in this thoughtful volume on the architectural examples to be found in Annapolis.

Upon reading the text and studying most carefully the illustrations of this volume it has occurred to me that here in Annapolis was born and developed and proved a truly American style—most happily suited to the American taste of today.

This happened because of various influences—for one that of climate—a varied one yet one without the intense winters of the north or the prolonged summers of the south. For another, a community built around the seat of government of the state and with an important hand in the founding of the National Government. A community closely knit with both academic education as well as the founding and training of a Navy for National defense and international good will long fostered at the Academy—and again, a long sustained pattern of the most important factor, life in the home.

As we stand looking about us for the next direction in architecture we look back on the immediate past to find that in the last few decades we have run the gamut of all schools, all national styles of architecture—including modern.

If we drive through any subdivision which has been developed in any American city within the last twenty-five years we find proof of this in the actual approximated examples of all schools of architecture—i.e. homes designed in the Tudor manner, the French Provincial, the Italian, the Swiss Chalet, etc., etc., as well as adaptations of our own regional styles, the Cape Cod salt box, the Hacienda, the Colonial (a miniature Mt. Vernon) and of course the Modern. All of these have been tested including the Modern which I stress as it is a style which has come into the field industrially as well as in domestic use and has proved to be in many cases an answer, in the former field especially, to a problem which has not previously existed. But I include Modern in the list of the styles tested since the turn of the century, for I feel that Modern has now taken its place in our national idiom and has now taken its place in architectural archives from which we may choose in the future. The one great flaw in Modern architecture for domestic living is that its promulgators have excluded in its prescribed furnishings everything of the past and thereby excluded any expression or intimation of the background of the inhabitants.

Therefore in contemplating this present volume of Annapolis homes I prefer to think of them as homes rather than houses. I am struck with the idea that here is a hand-book to point a true direction for a very real choice in the future of our domestic living. These homes were built with great thought and feeling by their future inhabitants and with the close interpretation of the owner's ideas by the architect. They were, to be sure, basically inspired by a style, contemporary in England at that time but so were *all our principles* based then; even while we, as a nation, were founding ourselves and proving our separate ideals. These homes have been inhabited ever since with minor changes and adaptations to the facts of climate and the changes in habits, and have been proved to be suited to our ways of life through many generations.

There are in this collection a variety of scaled houses each suited admirably to the varied size of family and the different scales of living today.

From the larger homes such as the symmetrically quiet and stately Hammond-Harwood House and the serenely spacious Chase House; through the friendly balanced dignity of the Brice, the Scott and the Ogle Houses; through the friendly compactness of the Windsor and Sands Houses to the disarming Aunt Lucy's Bake Shop itself. There is ample variety in scale for a choice based on premise of living in accordance with size of family, size of staff, size of plot and other aspects dictated by inclinations and income.

Whatever the size of the exterior there is, in all cases, an equal air of beauty and graciousness within. And whereas these houses are still (even after contemporary advantages of heating, lighting and improved functional arrangements) based on English inspiration—so is our national character. This is unquestionably true, because through trade and war we find ourselves now changed from foes to allies! and this despite some current political and international overtones.

Further—in examination of the many styles which have been tested in recent years, we find that our architectural flights into the continental styles have been none too contagious—either domestically or industrially and as for Modern, I fear the moderns protest too much for their style if it were on its way to becoming the national favorite.

In any case, let us at least consider the homes in this volume from the point of view that they are excellent examples of what is best suited to American living and psychology and therefore a true and tried pattern for the homes which are soon to be built.

In studying the text and illustrations of this volume it becomes apparent very soon that William Buckland, to whom most of these homes can assuredly be attributed, while founded in traditions of English architecture and while he kept himself informed regarding contemporary English developments; nevertheless he early formed a new expression, especially in his conception of the exterior of these homes in America. There is a cubic integrity of the whole which is uniquely American, and far from the exterior pretentiousness of many of the

English houses. Within, Buckland developed a school of ornamentation which was equally original in that it was both more daring and more delicately defined than the styles then in vogue in England. It might be said that he was even prophetic in his combining the motives of England, the Continent and the East in a way to produce an harmonious whole in the way that, in later years, our citizenship was to evolve from a combination of all the countries of the world.

Be that as it may, he evolved a beauty in interior design which was perhaps more in keeping with the life at that time in his own locale, than it is with life today. Still his exterior design is most suited to the taste of today and the American landscape especially and his interior design is still highly adaptable to interior design today in many ways such as stair cases, chimney pieces, door and window trim and in more formal instances, exactly suited to living as well as furnishing.

There is, both within and without a certain friendliness which I can best define in the cleanness of his line as emphasized in the forthrightness of his proportion. It is these proportions which are so satisfying to place pieces of good furniture against—the well designed pieces which were as honest then as they are functional today. There is space within the rooms—large or small—for the distribution of colour in a pleasing and architectural way and the scale of these rooms either with or without his more elaborate carvings, cornices and doorheads—take today the advantages of skillful contemporary lighting with a rewarding grace which probably surpasses the vagaries of candle light.

And finally there are advantages in the original lay-outs, with their thought for privacy (as opposed to a recent theory of all rooms opening-one-into-the-other!) that should be more welcome today when life is so involved, than they were during the times for which they were *first* designed!

And so having considered what is possibly the solution to an imminent problem we have gone further and discovered a character, William Buckland, new to most of us—a character by the proof of his works, more than by what we know of him, who came to this country in search of new opportunities, made his place as a citizen and should now be given his place as an outstanding figure among the many in our history who have given of themselves and their talents and thereby enriched the pattern of the true American way of life.

JOSEPH MULLEN,
A. I. D.

William Buckland by Charles Wilson Peale

18

WILLIAM BUCKLAND

POVERTY of definite knowledge concerning the professional architects, master builders or undertakers, (all were more or less synonymous in the Colonial Period) constitutes a sad gap in our national cultural background. In 1933 the late Dr. R. T. H. Halsey writing the foreword for the magnificent first volume of "Great Georgian Houses of America" made the same observation but added that diligent research would undoubtedly bring more information to light. Dr. Halsey goes on to state his discoveries and thoughtful deductions concerning one William Buckland, the subject of this chapter. The prediction that specific data on other Colonial architects would be unearthed has been verified by the evidence concerning John Ariss which Thomas Tileston Waterman has produced and set forth so interestingly in his latest book, "The Mansions of Virginia," University of North Carolina Press, Chapel Hill, N. C., 1946.

In research work of this kind the main sources of information are: authentic documentary evidence, and observations by experts from physical material. The true expert can accurately state with amazing exactness by whom and when a specific work was accomplished. Courts of law in making decisions involving vast sums of money have often been completely guided by the opinion of acknowledged authorities in the fields of paintings, antique furniture, etc. There are a few, perhaps half a dozen in the whole world, students of architecture whose findings from the physical evidence of a given structure would be equally accurate.

One of this group, Mr. Waterman, in writing of that most important architectural work, Mt. Airy, states that the carved cornice in the one section of the Mansion left intact by the disastrous fire which burned most of the magnificent interior in 1840 seemed very like the work of William Buckland as it appears in the superb wood trim of Gunston Hall. Documentary evidence recently brought forth at least a year after Mr. Waterman wrote the above shows that Buckland after completing Gunston Hall moved to the vicinity of Mt. Airy where he lived for the next ten years. Furthermore, the known dates for the completion of Gunston Hall and Mt. Airy would allow him to have worked on both.

The writer owes much to Mrs. Rosamond Randall Beirne and Mrs. Edith Rossiter Bevan, two eminent antiquarians, who have done an enormous amount of painstaking and intelligent research on Buckland and have discovered a wealth of most interesting material. Part of their findings may be found in the charming tiny volume, "The Hammond Harwood House," privately printed in 1941.

The Randalls are rightfully authorities on William Buckland, as their great grandfather, John Randall, of Richmond County, Virginia, having serious architectural ambitions, was at first apprenticed to Buckland, later became a junior partner and still later the executor of his estate. The Randalls possess a detail drawing of the bull's-eye window in the Hammond House executed by their ancestor and written evidence showing him to have worked on the old Senate Chamber in the State House. Lastly, those most rare and interesting documents, the indenture papers of William Buckland, are presently owned by this family. On the back of one of these documents in Buckland's own hand is a short personal history. He was born at Oxford, England, on August 14, 1734, bound apprentice to his uncle James Buckland in London, April 15, 1748, and came to Virginia with Thomson Mason, Esq., August 14, 1755. His London uncle was a master joiner, but, according to Mr. Halsey, was also the proprietor of the well-known book store in Pater Noster Row which specialized in the sale of architectural folios. Here young Buckland had not only practical training as an apprentice joiner but the opportunity to study a greater volume and variety of architectural designs than could in those days have been offered in any other manner. Judging from his work one can be sure that he made the most of these exceptional opportunities.

Mr. Halsey also contributes the following interesting observations concerning his practical training:

"Where Buckland obtained his builder's experience we do not know as yet. He may have done the joiner's work or had a chance to study carefully that beautiful Honington Hall in Warwickshire, 22 miles from Oxford, Buckland's home town—a Charles II house, remodelled just after the middle of the 18th Century by a wealthy London merchant, Joseph Townsend, and copiously illustrated in Volume V of Tipping's 'In English Homes.' A glance at the illustrations of Honington Hall shows us the stone quoins, the hexagonal porch with triglyphs which Buckland used in the frieze below the cornice of the rear porch (page 27) at Gunston Hall, as well as the elaborately carved modillions of the cornices in his Scott and Chase houses and Whitehall at Annapolis, and the octagonal extension which Buckland used in his addition to Ogle Hall in the same city.

The most assuring proof that Buckland must have known Honington Hall is to be seen in the elaborately carved panels of the interior shutters of its oak room, features most unusual if not unique in English houses. Rather similar ones are found in Buckland's Matthias Hammond house, Paca and Chase houses at Annapolis, but Buckland enriched his with large rosettes in relief in the center of each panel. Other unusual details which strengthen the argument are the highly carved window trim with the same 'ribband and flower' carvings in the salon of Honington Hall which Buckland used at the Matthias Hammond house, and the carved shutters and carved flattened corners of the window trim suggestive of those in the Chase house. The great doorways in the oak room may have suggested the similar but simplified ones at Whitehall. The oak leaves and acorns in the friezes are motifs Buckland used in the Paca house and Whitehall. The carved modillions of the pediment over the doors of the salon have the same bands of egg and dart and dental moldings as those on the great doorways of Whitehall. Another convincing proof of Buckland's knowledge of Honington Hall is the use of masks in the corners of the salon there. Buckland introduced carved masks in the corners of the coved ceiling at Whitehall. The incised line of carved ornament in the center of the doors themselves, used at Honington Hall is also found in two of Buckland's houses, Whitehall and the Chase House."

After completing Gunston Hall in 1759, there is a gap of three years before the next documentary records so far discovered show Buckland established in 1762 at Richmond County, Virginia, where the court records have many references to him as serving on juries, being hauled into court for swearing, etc. Here he married Mary Moore whose father William Moore was a man of importance.

Mr. Worth Bailey, curator at Mount Vernon and a student of architectural history, has suggested that Buckland may have done the interior woodwork of Old Polich Church which the masters of both Gunston Hall and Mount Vernon attended. The valuable church chronicles of Bishop Meade furnish this clue in recording that the original inside trim was inscribed "W. B." Documents have recently been uncovered which show that he made a mantelpiece for Robert Carter of Nomini and did some work for another member of this famous Virginia family. Moreover, court records prove that not all his labors were in the luxury field as they reveal that he built a jail in Richmond County. His outstanding abilities must have received ever increasing recognition and his work output must have been exceedingly large, as there are no less than thirty advertisements for different run-away indentured expert joiners or carvers. There is also record of three horses in Virginia belonging to him. One can easily picture Buckland riding from one client's home to another, throughout the Northern Neck of Virginia, with frequent trips by boat to Annapolis and perhaps even farther afield. Like a builder of today he without doubt had a small crew of his own expert workers at each project whose labors were supplemented by slaves from the owner's plantation rather than from the local union. His superb mantel, door and window frames were probably actually fashioned in his Virginia work shop and later shipped to their respective destinations.

The wording of Mason's letter of endorsement speaks most favorably of Buckland as a carpenter but makes no mention of his architectural ability and Gunston Hall is distinctly the earlier Virginia Wren or Queen Anne type except for its superb interior woodwork and the two entrance porches. This is easily understandable remembering that Buckland's indenture was for carpentering and joining and that he was only 21 years old at the start of his four years with Mason and a complete stranger in a strange land. However, his tremendous talents and obviously unusual training were soon recognized so that he became progressively more and more the designer until one may be sure that at least in the latest houses attributed to him he surely served as architect as well as in his original role of interior designer and master craftsman. In this connection it is interesting to note that the most fiercely modern architectural schools, Frank Lloyd Wright's and the Bauhaus, insist on the "new" idea that their students do actual hand labor in order to familiarize themselves with the true properties and limitations of their materials.

We presume Buckland brought some English architectural folios with him, but as court records show that at his death he possessed no less than 17 such volumes he must have kept adding to his collection by numerous shipments from his uncle's London book shop of the best and newest as soon as they became available. Among the books listed by his estate was the beautifully engraved and very costly "One Hundred and Fifty New Designs" by Thos. Johnson Carver, London, 1761. This date of publication proves that he must have received shipments after he arrived here. Further corroboration is at once discernible in his work. There are examples of decorative designs executed by him, obviously inspired from folio illustrations which were not published for ten years or more after his arrival in the Colonies, but which he used almost as soon as they appeared in London and sometime before their general acceptance in this country.

It is Buckland's work in Annapolis rather than in Virginia on which the major claims of his bid to enduring fame are based. To obtain the proper viewpoint on the importance of this work, one should visualize the city in the year 1774. There were approximately 450 houses, many of wood, and most of the others, very simple brick dwellings of modest size, such as Aunt Lucy's Bake Shop (page 114). Outstanding were a dozen or so magnificent estates standing on large plots with wonderful formal gardens, some terraced to the water. Of these mansions Buckland was presumably the architect of the six most impressive, and executed important additions to two of the others. Besides these town houses, he undoubtedly created Whitehall, the nearby country place of Maryland's Governor Sharp. This, the first Temple form dwelling in America, was the earliest of his completed works in the Annapolis sector, and undoubtedly its beauty plus the prominence of its owner caused all the ambitious aristocrats of neighboring Annapolis to vie with one another in obtaining Buckland's services. William Eddis, surveyor of customs writing in 1769 states: "The villas in the vicinity of Annapolis are pleasant and beautiful, especially Whitehall."

Benjamin Mifflin of Philadelphia in 1762 reported that "although there are several large buildings with Capacious Gardens, I did not see one with any degree of elegance or taste." The somewhat acid tone of these remarks may have been caused at least in part by the envy of Philadelphians for the lucrative shipping business enjoyed by Annapolis. Nevertheless from our knowledge of the structures standing at that time the writer feels that these unflattering comments must have been near the truth. Yet, a Frenchman writing of the Maryland Capital during the Revolution states "female luxury exceeds the Provinces of France. One woman pays her French hairdresser a thousand crowns per year. The State House is very beautiful, in fact, the most beautiful I have seen in America. Of its few (important) buildings at least three quarters may be styled elegant and grand."

The diary of the famous English traveler, and friend of George Washington, Samuel Vaughan, dated 1787 states, "The city contains about 450 houses, 2500 inhabitants, State House, Court House, Gaol, Church, Governor's House, poor house, playhouse, assembly room and the following gentlemen have superb houses that would not disgrace Westminister, Col. Edward Loyd, Mr. Hammond, Mr. Rydoubt, Mr.. Carrol, Mr. Davison, Mr. Harrold, Mr. Stone, Messrs. Wallace, Johnson, and Dr. Scott. Here, Mr. Mann keeps an excellent public house. Four rooms on a floor and one for company, 66 feet by 21 feet. The second story lodging rooms all wainscoted to the ceiling might vie with any tavern in England." The last two excerpts certainly more than make up for the unkind comments of Mr. Mifflin. Why such a complete reversal? The answer lies in the dates of these observations. The first was written in 1762 before Buckland and his artistry entered the picture. Could anything be more convincing proof of his profound influence?

There is very positive deductive and circumstantial evidence to presume that in the Maryland Capital he was responsible for the superb Chase, Paca, Scott and Ridout houses, the octagonal rear wing of Ogle Hall and the octagonal ball room wing of the Governor's House which formerly stood on what is now part of the United States Naval Academy grounds.

There is unassailable documentary proof showing William Buckland to be the architect of the Hammond-Harwood House. Page (18) is a photograph of a portrait of Buckland by Charles Wilson Peale. One can plainly see on the table a floor plan and elevation of the Hammond-Harwood House.

It is interesting to note that despite favorite local stories of a more sentimental nature, Peale's Diary states that this portrait started in 1773 was not completed until 1787. One wonders where the unfinished picture was during these fourteen years?

Mr. Halsey attributed the Brice House to Buckland and the physical evidence seemed indisputedly to substantiate this claim, but all other authorities placed the date of building as 1740, based on evidence showing that Edmund Jennings gave the place to his daughter, Juliana, as a wedding present on her marriage to Col. James Brice. The writer takes great satisfaction in being able to corroborate Mr. Halsey and the physical evidence for he recently found the following advertisement in a Maryland Gazette of 1773:

Patrick Tonry's Tavern situated in East Street a few doors below
Mr. James Brice's *new house*, near and convenient to the dock.

This coupled with the fact that the Randall family possess a bill for work done, rendered against Mr. Brice by the Buckland estate, and the physical evidence of the splendid interior and exterior wood trim surely leaves no doubt as to his participation in the present five part structure. It is possible that the center, or main house may incorporate an earlier simpler dwelling.

Buckland worked on the two most highly articulated examples of Colonial domestic architecture still remaining to us: The Hammond-Harwood House, 1774 of Annapolis, and Mount Airy, 1760 of Virginia. Most fortunately the Annapolis dwelling remains in a remarkably original state throughout. Prior to the Revolution there were, as far as is known in all the Colonies, only two other Mansions of equal architectural sophistication: *Roswell,* the Page homestead in Virginia, and *Tryon's Palace,* the Governor's House at New Bern, North Carolina. Tragically, fire has consumed both.

Perhaps Buckland's most outstanding design characteristic is daring. In an age of great conservatism he eagerly adopted whatever he liked from the newest fashion yet retained his former preferences as well. In this manner he created a minor style of his own. In the wood trim at Gunston Hall one sees Greek, Roman, Louis XV, and Chinese motifs freely intermingled, yet so skillfully blended that the result is completely smooth and absolutely unique.

An example of his daring is displayed in the use of different designs for each of the several pediments in the principal room of this house.

Thomas Chippendale, the greatest furniture designer of all time, employed the same melange of basic designs with the same unity of result. We know that Buckland owned a copy of Chippendale's famous "DIRECTOR" and that it was during his apprenticeship with his uncle in London that Chippendale attained an unique eminence. It is interesting to speculate on how much influence the great prestige of the furniture designer had on the budding architect who also is said to have produced some furniture, of which to the present time we have unfortunately found no examples.

At the Hammond House where Buckland was the complete architect his freedom of artistic creation is expressed in the building's very different street and garden facades as shown in pages (41, 48, 49). In his later work he added touches from the brothers Adam to the list of design sources mentioned in connection with Gunston Hall. His carving was superb, having a mastery of touch and finish comparable with the schools of Gibbons and Chippendale. Indeed an eminent English architect recently examining the entrance door of the Hammond-Harwood House was most insistent that it must have been made in London. So great was the beauty of the mansions he built, that their influence on others was far reaching.

If Buckland was the architect as well as Interior Designer of all the houses on which he worked, his variation in styles was extraordinary, ranging from the simple Virginia Colonial of Gunston Hall to the Palladian monumental plan of the Chase House, the Roman Villa derivation Hammond-Harwood House, and the Temple Dwelling—Whitehall.

The writer has a strong personal predilection for rooms fully paneled in wood. In this one respect Buckland is a great disappointment. None of the houses attributed to him employ this most beautiful of wall coverings. The Brice House has beveled edged panels in some of its rooms but they are mere imitations worked into the plaster. The reason for this departure from the full wainscot is that the fashion had passed its height in England when Buckland was serving his apprenticeship. His chair rail panels when of wood were of the plain sunken variety which was likewise the latest development but not nearly so rich in design value as the earlier beveled and fielded form.

In this respect, because of its earlier architectural style, Williamsburg surpasses Annapolis, as there are a number of fully paneled rooms still to be seen there, while in Maryland's Capital one can only find a single remaining example: The Great Hall in the Workman House. What a pity that the wainscoting mentioned by Vaughan in the Mann Tavern, formerly the Daniel Dulaney Mansion, has disappeared.

There has recently been found a plan of the Hammond-Harwood House by Thomas Jefferson who must have much admired its unusual architectural qualities as he used its octagonal ends at Monticello. Moreover, it was at Whitehall where he first saw the temple form employed in domestic architecture. So profound was his impression that he employed this feature not only at Monticello but in so many other structures whose architectural form he influenced, that Jefferson's sponsoring of this design has made it our best known National style.

Coming to America as an indentured man and dying at the tragically early age of forty, William Buckland, nevertheless, in his 19 years as a Colonial, besides producing the artistic work herein mentioned, had attained the rank of gentleman and amassed a considerable fortune as is shown in contemporary court records. It is interesting to note that this was prior to the Revolution. His daughter married John Callahan, Registrar of the Land Office, and his granddaughter through her marriage with Richard Harwood became mistress of the Hammond-Harwood House, his superb final achievement.

What could be greater proof of true democracy and just reward for outstanding ability, intelligence and courage? Buckland almost unknown to the rank and file of today, is surely one of a magic group of Americans who are the true founders of our National Architectural and Artistic Culture.

23

The Garden Facade

GUNSTON HALL
Circa 1754-58

Thompson Mason, studying law in London, brought young Buckland back with him as an indentured carpenter and joyner to work on this proposed house of his famous patriot brother, George Mason. Despite its simple exterior probably no house in America has ever had greater originality or elaboration of detail in its interior design.

The Northern Facade of Gunston Hall

GUNSTON HALL
Circa 1754-58

Although this Virginia Estate's inclusion in a volume on Annapolis may seem an anachronism it deserves its place as the first thoroughly authenticated work of William Buckland whose influence on the Colonial architecture of Annapolis was so profound.

A detail of the Northern Facade Porch

A detail of the Garden Facade Porch

Photograph: Courtesy of Russell Whitehead

The Entrance Hall

Photograph: Courtesy of Russell Whitehead

Staircase Detail

Photograph: Courtesy of Russell Whitehead

A Drawing Room Window Detail

The Drawing Room Doorway

31

Photograph: Courtesy of Russell Whitehead

A Corner Cupboard in the Drawing Room

The walls covered in simple unpaneled pine sheathing were never meant to be left bare as shown. They were originally covered in chintz, toille, or damask.

Photograph: Courtesy of Russell Whitehead

A detail of the Corner Cupboard Entablature

33

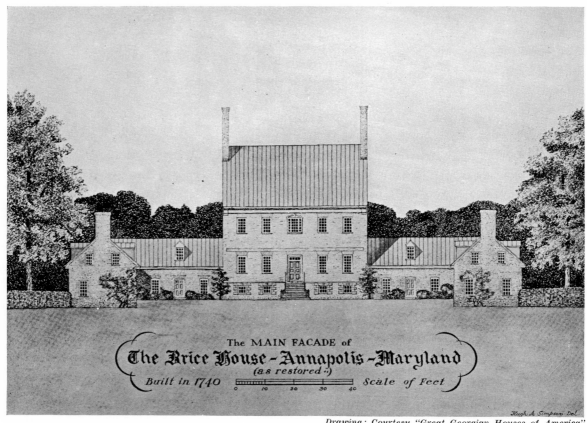

The MAIN FACADE of
𝕿𝖍𝖊 𝕭𝖗𝖎𝖈𝖊 𝕳𝖔𝖚𝖘𝖊 ~ 𝕬𝖓𝖓𝖆𝖕𝖔𝖑𝖎𝖘 ~ 𝕸𝖆𝖗𝖞𝖑𝖆𝖓𝖉
(as restored)
Built in 1740   Scale of Feet
0   10   20   30   40

Hugh A. Simpson Del.

Drawing: Courtesy "Great Georgian Houses of America"

The Street Entrance Facade of the James Brice House

THE BRICE HOUSE
Circa 1772

This was built for Col. John Brice who married Juliana Jennings in 1742. The house is presently owned by St. John's College and used as a residence for faculty members. This is one of the places for which there is documentary as well as physical evidence showing that William Buckland was the Master Builder. Its plan is very similar to the nearby Paca House, but its gabled roof is almost medieval in its great unbroken height. In strong contrast is the unusually elaborate and sophisticated cornice, page 36. Legend has it that Edmund Jennings gave the house to his daughter as a wedding present. If this is true, Buckland may have incorporated this older dwelling into the present mansion.

The Street Facade of the Main House

Window and Cornice Detail

Photograph: Courtesy of Russell Whitehead

The Living Room Doorway

Photograph: Courtesy of Russell Whitehead

The Living Room Mantel

The Fireplace Wall in the Southwest Room

THE · STREET · FACADE
THE · MATTHIAS · HAMMOND · HOUSE
· Annapolis · Maryland ·
Built in 1770 ~ William · Buckland · Architect
NOW OWNED BY ST. JOHNS COLLEGE AS A COLONIAL MUSEUM
Graphic Scale

Rendering Courtesy: "Great Georgian Houses of America"

HAMMOND-HARWOOD HOUSE
Circa 1774

This is the final and crowning architectural achievement of William Buckland who died just prior to its completion.

Matthias Hammond, a young lawyer, ordered the dwelling on becoming engaged. There are many local legends, the best authenticated of which is that his fiancee, a Miss Chase, eloped with another man while Hammond was in Philadelphia ordering furniture for his Mansion.

The street entrance facade of the Hammond-Harwood House

HAMMOND-HARWOOD HOUSE
Circa 1774

Hammond never lived in the house but it had many distinguished owners as well as falling on hard times before being taken over recently by the Hammond-Harwood House Committee.

This most worthy organization is presently exerting every effort to effect a perfect restoration. The place is open to the public and should be a "must" on every American sightseeing list, as it is without doubt one of the finest medium sized houses of the world and almost unique for its practically original condition.

The Great Doorway of the Oak Room at Honington Hall near Oxford, England, where Buckland is presumed to have done his apprentice work.

The Entrance of the Hammond-Harwood House

The carving is of extraordinary beauty and sophistication.

43

Photograph: Courtesy of Russell Whitehead

Detail of Entablature

Entrance Doorway

Photograph: Hayman Studio

The second floor hall window with beautifully carved bull's eye above

The Garden Facade

Photograph: Hayman Studio

Note the complete difference from the entrance facade in architectural style and detail. This elevation is almost Queen Ann in character.

Detail of link between main house and wing, street facade

Photograph: Courtesy of Russell Whitehead

Detail of Stairway Window

Garden Doorway

Garden Doorway

Detail of Entablature

Garden Facade

Detail of link between Main House and Wing

The extremely simple Entrance Hall

Photograph: Courtesy Russell Whitehead

The stairway is separate from and to the right of the Entrance Hall

54

Front Drawing Room

Detail of simple mantel

The lovely small mantel in Front East Parlor

Photograph: Courtesy Russell Whitehead

Detail of mantel carving

South Wall of the Grand Dining Room

Photograph: Courtesy Russell Whitehead

The North Wall of the Grand Dining Room

A Salon Window at Honington Hall near Oxford, England

A Corner of the Grand Dining Room at Hammond-Harwood House

Here Buckland has improved on the shutter decoration of the English mansion.

Photograph: Courtesy Russell Whitehead

Detail of the Grand Dining Room Chimney Piece

Cornice of the Grand Dining Room

Photograph: Hayman Studio

Doorway of the Grand Dining Room

Photograph: Courtesy Russell Whitehead

Detail of the Grand Dining Room Doorway

Cornice and Mantel of the **Second Floor** Music Room which overlooks the Garden

Photograph: Courtesy Russell Whitehead

Kitchen, West Wing, in remarkably original condition

WHITEHALL
Circa 1766

This house, located five miles north of Annapolis and built circa 1766 for Royal Governor Horatio Sharp, is particularly remarkable architecturally for two features. It was the first temple form dwelling in America and in a remarkably "Modern" manner was so constructed on rising ground that its entrance facade is one full story higher than the garden side. The present roof line has been heightened and the arcaded connecting links added since the original building date. The main house follows the Maryland custom of one room depth so as to make the greatest use of cooling breezes.

The Governor planned the place as a summer seat but on his retirement from office in 1769 lived there the year round until he returned to England in 1773. He entertained lavishly and set the pace for the social whirl of the nearby capital.

Sharp died in England in 1790 willing Whitehall to John Ridout.

A superb view of Whitehall showing the Temple Form of its Garden Entrance Porch. The roof line of the Main House has been raised.

The magnificent Entrance Hall

The wood trim is particularly fine.

Detail of Mantelpiece

The insert is a detail of the elaborately carved mask inset at the corner of the high ceiling cove.

Some of Buckland's splendid carving on the window frames in the Dining Room

Photograph: Hayman Studio

The wood trim of the Sitting Room windows is very similar though not as elaborate

Photograph: Hayman Studio

The charming simple mantel of the sitting room

A very fine small block front chest and other fine furniture of the period in a bedroom

THE RIDOUT HOUSE
Circa 1770

John Ridout came from England with Horatio Sharp and at once became a man of importance as the secretary and close friend of this Royal Governor. Remarkably the friendship survived young Ridout's winning the contest between them for the hand of Mary Ogle, the lovely daughter of the former Governor, for Sharp willed beautiful "Whitehall" to the Ridouts. The physical evidence plainly shows that Ridout followed his patron in choosing Buckland as his architect.

This splendid example of a Georgian dwelling has remained through the years in the hands of the Ridout family.

A detail of the Entrance Door

The unfortunate hand rail is of much later date.

Photograph: Hayman Studio

The Entrance Facade

The Garden Elevation

79

Garden Elevation of the Dr. Upton Scott House

THE SCOTT HOUSE
Circa 1768

Dr. Upton Scott also came to Annapolis from England in 1759 with Governor Horatio Sharp as the latter's personal physician.

Conceding that Governor Sharp employed Buckland for his superb country place, *Whitehall,* it would seem most likely that Dr. Scott would follow the taste dictates of the Governor by commissioning the same builder. The superb woodwork of the house supports this supposition.

The Entrance Facade

THE SCOTT HOUSE
Circa 1768

The present coat of grey paint is a later and unfortunate addition. Francis Scott Key, the grand nephew of the Doctor lived here while studying at St. John's college.

The Main Stairway with typically superlative Buckland carving

Detail of the Main Hall

THE CHASE-LLOYD HOUSE

Samuel Chase, one of the signers of the Declaration of Independence, ordered the construction of this house in 1769 but in 1771 it was sold though only partially finished to Edward Lloyd, later Governor of the State. Completed in 1774, credit for its unusual and magnificent interior should go to Mr. Lloyd who presumably employed Buckland to add the superb finishing touches which make the mansion so outstanding. Buckland was at the same time working on the Hammond-Harwood House, directly across the street.

Mrs. Hester Ann Chase Ridout, the last private owner, left the place to the Protestant Episcopal Church in 1897.

The Chase-Lloyd House

Corner of Maryland Avenue and King George Street
Annapolis, Maryland

The superb Entrance Hall and Stairs

The landing of the Main Stairway

THE PACA HOUSE
Circa 1770

The Mansion was built for William Paca, one of the signers of the Declaration of Independence and third elected Governor of Maryland in 1782. It is now a part of "Carvel Hall" an hotel so called because it was the house used as background in Winston Churchill's novel of that name.

The garden facade has been altered beyond all recognition by a very large addition painted yellow. The entrance side, page 89, still shows the lovely natural brick color, a few old irregular window lights in their old muntons and retains in general its original appearance. However, the roof line of the hyphens has been raised; the gabled roof of one of the dependencies changed to the hip variety, and other unfortunate innovations both inside and out have occurred.

Of the original interior there remains only a small room directly to the left of the entrance in which one may see shutters and mantel, of superbly carved wood, page 90. These together with the handsome plaster cornice mouldings and over mantel picture-frame speak eloquently of William Buckland's artisanship.

It is to be hoped that in the near future a truly fine job of restoration and repair will be done on this beautiful and historic building.

The entrance facade as it now appears

Photograph: Hayman Studio

The only room of the Paca House which contains its original trim. The cornice is of plaster as is the picture-frame. However, the carved wooden mantel and window shutters are typical of Buckland.

90

OGLE HALL
Circa 1740

Samuel Ogle, three times Provincial Governor of Maryland, ordered this town house built about 1740. His Manorial Estate was "Belaire," now on the main highway to the Nation's Capital and presently beautifully restored and maintained by William Woodward, three times winner of the Kentucky Derby.

Governor Ogle, too, was a great horse lover with his own track at Belaire and famous imported blood stock. At one time he had English deer sent to his park at the Manor. When 47 he married beautiful 18-year-old Anne Tasker who undoubtedly enjoyed the town house and the gaiety it offered.

The dwelling has recently been purchased and a most intelligent and careful restoration work is being done. There is a new addition to the Eastern end of the house but as it is set back from the original facade, one is not too conscious of it. The small balcony on the second floor at the west is of a later date and of course the present rather attractively faded grey paint was not applied in Governor Ogle's time.

The octagonal rear wing is attributed to William Buckland.

Photograph: Hayman Studio

Entrance facade of the Ogle Mansion

The balcony visible through the tree fork is a later addition.

Entrance to the Octagonal Ball Room Wing which projects from the Garden Facade

This wing is attributed to Buckland.

Drawing: Courtesy "Great Georgian Houses of America"

MONTPELIER
Circa 1751 and circa 1770

This country Manor, though a number of miles from Annapolis, the central portion of which was built for Nicholas Snowden in 1751 and in 1770 enlarged for the son, Major Thomas Snowden, is included in this volume because some noted authorities believe Buckland to have been responsible for the added hyphens and wings.

If not actually the master's work, their octagonal plan and interior details certainly could fairly be called of the Buckland school. The Manor has been beautifully restored and furnished by Mr. and Mrs. Breckenridge Long.

Photograph: Courtesy Russell Whitehead

The West Entrance

The similarity between this door and that of the Ogle House, page 93, strengthens the supposition that Buckland worked here.

Photograph: Courtesy Russell Whitehead

The East Doorway

Photograph: Courtesy Russell Whitehead

The view through the East Doorway

The First Floor Hall

This, the Main Hall, was built before Buckland came to the Colonies but is shown as a beautiful example of an earlier style.

Photograph: Courtesy Russell Whitehead

A detail of the stairway

A beautiful simple early design with no carving

Photograph: Courtesy Russell Whitehead

The First Floor Southeast Drawing Room

Photograph: Courtesy Russell Whitehead

More fine antiques and the window of the Southeast Drawing Room, formerly the Dining Room

The China Closet in the Southeast Drawing Room

Photograph: Courtesy Russell Whitehead

Detail of the China Closet Entablature in the older portion of the house

This crude carving could never have emanated from Buckland's shop.

Photograph: Courtesy Russell Whitehead

The Second Floor Hall

Photograph: Courtesy Russell Whitehead

The Mantel in the Northeast Bed Room

McDOWELL HALL
1742

The history of this large square hip-roofed brick building began more than two hundred years ago.

In 1742, the Maryland Assembly authorized Governor Thomas Bladen to buy four acres of land and build "a Dwelling House and other Conveniences for the Residence of the Governor of Maryland for the time being." The cost was not to exceed £4000. A Scotch builder, Simon Duff, was employed and work begun. After two years a request to the Assembly for £2000 more to complete the project was refused.

Benjamin Mifflin, a Philadelphian, wrote after visiting Annapolis in 1762: "Viewed Bladen's Folly as the Inhabitants call it, the ruins of a Spacious Building begun by Governor Bladen but carried no further than the Brick Work and Joists two Stories High, but if finished would have been a Beautiful Edifice."

When St. John's College was chartered in 1784, it acquired Bladen's Folly and completed the project naming it McDowell Hall in honor of the college's first President. George Washington sent his two nephews Fairfax and Lawrence Washington there in 1794 and in 1798, Mrs. Washington's grandson, George Washington Parke Custis attended. Francis Scott Key was another early graduate. In 1909 a disastrous fire destroyed all but the walls of the old building. However, it has been ably restored.

Bladen's Folly or McDowell Hall

STATE HOUSE

The first state house, called Stadt House in deference to Dutch King William, was erected in 1697. Destroyed by fire in 1706, it was re-erected in similar form and using the original walls. W. Bladen was the contractor, receiving £1000 for the work. It was "a neat brick oblong building" according to contemporary description. After 65 years the structure was so run down it became "an emblem of public poverty." With their natural pride in Annapolis aroused, the inhabitants planned an ambitious edifice and in 1772 employed Joseph Clark to create the work. There have been many additions and changes through the years, but recently the old pre-Revolutionary Senate Chamber was most ably restored to its Colonial appearance. The first meeting of the Continental Congress was held in this room. Here, too, in 1783, George Washington resigned his commission as commander-in-chief, and in January, 1784, the Treaty of Peace with Great Britain signed in Paris the previous September, was ratified by the new Congress of the United States.

Contemporary portraits of William Paca and Samuel Chase of Annapolis, whose homes are herein depicted, hang here together with those of many other great Colonial figures including LaFayette and George Washington.

On the lawn are statues of famous historical figures, and one of the cannon from the Ark and Dove, the two small ships which brought English colonists to Maryland in 1634.

The State House

The dome, a late and ponderous addition, has been removed in this photograph to give a truer picture of its original appearance.

ACTON

Acton, Annapolis, Maryland

This red brick dwelling was built for Philip Hammond, a relative of Matthias Hammond. The hyphen and wing appear to be of later date and should be balanced with a similar addition on the other side.

Photograph: Hayman Studio

The Entrance Facade

REYNOLDS TAVERN

The all header bond brick work of the entrance facade and its unusual arched string courses serve as excellent examples of the great care and architectural detail lavished on the fine early taverns of America. This hostelry has as its guests all the great names of 18th Century Marylanders and Virginians together with many from the other colonies as well as English and Continental travelers. Mann's Hotel, which finally surpassed it in magnificence, was not opened until just after the Revolution and unfortunately is now destroyed.

The Annapolis Public Library presently occupies Reynolds.

The Entrance Facade of the Reynolds Tavern

Note the arched string course and all header bond brick.

Aunt Lucy's Bake Shop

A perfect prototype for the low informal home so much sought after today. The original
brick color is hidden by a coat of yellow paint.

THE CARROLL-McCANDLESS HOUSE, circa 1730

Living Room Mantel in the oldest portion of the residence c. 1730. The plot on which this house stands shows on the original Plat of Annapolis as belonging to James Carroll of the famous Maryland family bearing that name. Later it passed into the hands of the McCandless family. About 1830 the dwelling was greatly enlarged. Paul Mellon, son of Andrew Mellon, while a student at St. John's had the house charmingly restored for his occupancy. Mr. and Mrs. Stringfellow Barr are now in residence there. Mr. Barr is the famous president of St. John's.

The Old Treasury and Council Chamber
Circa 1695

This cruciform brick building was originally the Council Chamber. From 1837 to 1903 it served as the State Treasury. The beautiful true brick color has been painted over and many other unfortunate changes made, especially in its interior. However, this facade is very near its original appearance.

Windsor House, circa 1760

The typical Gambrel Roof and wide hand beaded boards of the pre-Revolution Maryland House is perfect for today as well as then. Originally built for Reverdy Johnson, the house stood on North West Street until 1940 when it was moved to its present site on the College Green just off St. John's street.

The Sands House, circa 1680, with numerous later additions and changes.

It is still in the Sands family and contains many momentoes of interest and some original furniture.

The Green House, circa 1690

Its low Gambrel Roof and wing at the rear make it a fine design source. The shed roof dormers are interesting. The siding is new.

BIBLIOGRAPHY

A PARTIAL LIST of the many sources used in the author's research is listed. His debts are gratefully acknowledged to the authors of the following:

Annals of Annapolis. David Ridgely.
Annapolis, Its Colonial and Naval Story. Walter B. Norris.
Annapolis, Anne Arundel's Towne. William Oliver Stevens.
Annapolis. Elmer Martin Jackson.
Annapolis on the Severn. Monograph Series, Volume 16.
History of Annapolis. O. M. Taylor.
Guide to Annapolis. Trader and Sturdy.
Letters from America. William Eddis.
Historical Notices of St. Ann's Parish. Rev. Ethan Allen.
The Hammond-Harwood House. Monograph Series, Volume 15.
Great Georgian Houses of America. Foreword by R. T. H. Halsey.
Tidewater Maryland. Paul Wilstach.
Homes of the Cavaliers. Katherine Scarborough.
Archives of Maryland.
The Maryland Gazette.
The Virginia Gazette.
The Maryland Historical Magazine.
The Hammond-Harwood House and Its Owners. Rosamond Randall Beirne and Edith Rossiter Bevan.

ANNAPOLIS STRUCTURES
Erected Prior to 1776 and Still Extant

THE FOLLOWING LIST of structures erected in Annapolis before 1776 is submitted to show the volume of early American building still standing in the city and to offer a concise guide to those who wish to see its fine old houses.

It must be emphasized that while there has been a sincere effort to make it complete, in a project of this sort, there are inevitably unintentional omissions. The facades of many older houses were so altered during the Victorian era as to make their actual period unrecognizable to the passerby. Unless unlimited time is available, one making such a survey must depend to some extent upon the guidance and assistance of residents of the town under consideration. Without knowing it, he is almost certain to miss out-of-the-way examples in covering such a sizeable area with a very considerable grid of streets. Also in the case of small wooden structures of "tenement" type, alterations and replacements have been more easily made and often have concealed their true age.

Acton House	1760	
Assembly Rooms	1764	City Hall
Aunt Lucy's Bake Shop	1765	160 Prince George
Bordley-Randall House	1735	Randall Court
Bowie Mansion		(now Maryland Hotel)
James Brice House	1740–42	Prince George & East Sts.
Brooksbury-Shaw House	1720	(now Elks Club)
Callahan Pinkney House	1740	131 Charles St.
Carroll House	1735	St. Mary's Church Grounds
Carroll-McCandless House	1702–18	139 Market St.
		(originally Carroll House on 1717 map.)
Caton's Barber Shop		Market Place (George Washington used it)
Chase-Lloyd House	1769	22 Maryland Ave., N.W. Corner King George
Davison Tydings House	1722	N.W. Corner, Main and Conduit
Dulaney-Duvall House	1730	179 Duke of Gloucester
Forensic Club	1770	170 Duke of Gloucester
Green House	1680	124 Charles Street
Hammond-Harwood House	1770–74	21 Maryland Ave.
Jennings House	1685	195 Prince George
Lloyd-Dulaney House	1770	162 Conduit St.
MacCubbin House	1740	193 Main St.
McDowell Hall (Bladen's Folly)	1744–84	Campus Green & College Ave.
Morehead-Dorsey House	1694	211 Prince George
Ogle Mansion	1737	33 College Ave.
Old Treasury	1694	State House Circle
Paca House	1763	192 Prince George
Peggy Stewart House	1763	207 Hanover St.
Pinkney-Carpenter House	1750	5 St. Johns St. (moved here in 1905)
Quynn House	1750	9 Northwest St.

Reynolds Tavern	1737	Church Circle
Ridout House	1763–65	120 Duke of Gloucester
Sands House	1680	130 Prince George St. (oldest frame)
Scott House	1770	4 Shipwright
Slicer House	1740	Taylor St.
State House	1772–93	State House Circle
Tilton House	1750	9 Maryland Ave.
Walton-Workman House	1696	10 Francis St.
Windsor House	1730	Campus Green & St. John's St.